Move Over Satan You're In My Seat

by

David R. High

Books for Children of the World

6701 N. Bryant,

Oklahoma City, OK 73121

ISBN 0-9661186-1-8

Distributed by:
Books for Children of the World
6701 N. Bryant
Oklahoma City, OK 73121
voice - 405/721-7417
fax - 405/478-4352

Cover & Illustrations by:
Justin Bonnema
Legacy Productions
7004 Sanders Ln.
Plano, TX 75025

Editor's Note:

All Scriptures are King James version. Underlining and parenthesis are author's for emphasis or for explanation. Scripture pronouns and pronoun/noun-verb agreement were changed to modern English for easier reading. Pronouns for deity were capitalized. Scripture punctuation was left in the King James version.

Printed in the United States of America

Table of Contents

Introduction

At some point in eternity past, the heart of God conceived man. In His creation plan, God chose man to occupy a special position. Conferred upon man was a position of close fellowship and extended rulership with God Himself. As far as we know, none other of God's creation has ever enjoyed such a lofty position.

Unfortunately, due to man's failure to properly grasp his opportunity, or should we say his responsibility, this divine communion between God and man was spoiled. God had a job for man to do. These questions remain before us: What was Adam's appointed task? Did he succeed or fail? If he failed, what was his job and can someone else still do it? If the job is yet to be done and someone can do it, what will happen then?

You see, man was not the only one who suffered loss at the fall. We will discover that when man failed, God lost and so did all of creation. God wanted things back the way they were so much that He was willing to sacrifice His own Son to set things in order again. You are a creature of divine destiny. Our heavenly Father has already set things in motion to change your life forever.

A thorough detective in his attempt to solve a crime searches carefully for clues surrounding the event that will enable him to see that truth prevails. If we are willing to become thorough detectives of the Scriptures, many wonders that are yet to be revealed will become our evidence of the truth God has for us. Once you are on the trail of revelation knowledge, you begin to see God's fingerprints everywhere. It is as if He is encouraging us in our search by showing us more and more pieces of His heavenly mystery.

Let us through the Scriptures discover who we really are. Once you have a clear picture of your destiny, you will discover that you have more to contribute to God's future plans than you could ever have imagined. I write this with the prayer that these discoveries will leave you forever changed and challenged to invest the rest of your life in this glorious quest.

Chapter I

Adam's Authority Versus Abraham's Promises

If you have known the Lord any time at all, I am sure you would agree that we certainly need God's help to live a victorious life. Our own skills, training, and capabilities seem frail when we attempt in our own strength to stand against the wiles of the devil. The good news is that God not only wants us to be overcomers but has made provision for us to be overcomers.

Imagine that some great personal struggle has come your way and you were able to visit heaven and personally make your request for help to God Himself. God looks at you and says, "I have already made provision for you at Calvary. Choose one of the two doors before you. Take all the provisions you find inside and go forward to victory."

You stand before two great doors knowing that you can choose only one. One door is marked "Adam's Authority" and the other is marked "Abraham's

Promises." Think carefully before you choose because you may have only one.

Before you choose, however, be aware of this: The Scriptures tell us that as a man thinks in his heart, so is he. What we believe to be true about ourselves molds and shapes our self-image and subsequent actions. Identifying with one covenant does not eliminate the other, but it diminishes its influence. What you think about the most has the most influence.

For years the Church has, by emphasis, spent most of its time at the door of Abraham's promises.

> **Now the Lord had said to Abram, "Get you out of your country, and from your kindred, and from your father's house, unto a land that I will show you: And I will make of you a great nation, and I will bless you, and make your name great; and you shall be a blessing: And I will bless them who bless you, and curse him who curses you, and in you shall all families of the earth be blessed."**
>
> **Genesis 12:1-3**

Abraham's covenant is primarily one that pursues and distributes blessing.[1]

---

[1] **You must forgive me if during our discovery some points are slightly overstated or oversimplified. Please resist the temptation to pick apart the finer points of my theology and try to grasp the bigger picture. While you may disagree with some conclusions, at least think with me about the possibilities.**

If the majority of your Christian experience revolves around being blessed and being a blessing, it is easy to see how some could drift toward the being blessed side. While not wanting to be critical, it seems that much of the focus of the modern church is on the "benefits" of tithing, getting prayer answered, getting healed, beating up on the devil, etc. All of these things are both important and necessary, but are they the best and highest?

Answer this question: Did Jesus die to give you Abraham's promises or Adam's authority? I think any Bible reading Christian would eventually have to come to the conclusion that Calvary bought back for us what Adam lost. Just what was the provision of Calvary? ICor. 15:45 says that Jesus was the last Adam, not the last Abraham. Abraham didn't lose anything; he was the beneficiary of a covenant.

To make an intelligent, informed decision about who you are as the redeemed, some more information is needed. That, after all, is the essence of the word redeem (to buy back). If Jesus died to give back to me all that Adam was, how can I ever know who by Calvary I am to be if I have no idea who Adam was before sin? God may have well been offering us a higher self-image through the cross than we ever realized. Before you choose your one and only door, let's see if we can learn more about who Adam was.

Chapter II

God's Plan from the Beginning

What was this world really like before sin? How often I have dreamed of a world void of war, hunger, sickness, and poverty. As people struggle with the complexities of our modern society, the old question inevitably arises: If there is a loving God, why do people starve to death? People want to blame God for everything. I hope to show you that social problems are not God's fault. In the beginning, God created a perfect world and there were none of the global problems we face today. There were no starving masses in Somalia. There were no oppressive governments. Mankind never knew sickness or hatred. Nature wasn't polluted by man's excesses. God created a perfect environment and placed in it a perfect man to rule it as His representative.

In Adam's world, the bugs didn't destroy the fruit, storms didn't destroy the wheat, floods didn't cover the fields; rather, nature was subject to man because man was subject to God. In this pre-sin world, all the living systems were in such balance that God intended for man to live forever in harmony with his surroundings.

> **And God saw every thing that He had made, and, behold, it was very good.**
>
> **Genesis 1:31**

The reality, however, is that sin did come into our world and the chaotic conditions of our modern society have created cause after cause that demands our attention. What should we do about the whales, acid rain, global warming, polluted water, toxic food supplies, the rain forest, toxic dumps, nuclear weapons, run-away governments, eroding morals, divorce, drugs, crime, abortion, drive-by shootings, and terrorism? Open your newspaper to any page and you will find something to stir your emotions and challenge your sense of righteousness and justice. With all the glaring problems our world faces today, it is difficult at times to imagine that first perfect world so balanced that none of these subjects would have ever come up, much less totally preoccupy our thoughts. In Adam's world, he slept peacefully at night. He loved his wife and she loved him. They never worried about their next meal. No thief stole their possessions. This fine-tuned environment worked flawlessly because it had the life of God flowing through it. What a place! What a time!

Not only did Adam have the privilege of living in a perfect place, but he also walked and talked with a perfect God. Before sin, God would give instruction to Adam, and under God's authority, Adam would rule. Before sin, there is no evidence that Adam had any trouble with the animals, the weather, or his marriage. Order flowed and peace ruled.

Adam also had a perfect body. Is it possible that man could live forever in a human body and never die? In the beginning, that was God's plan. If sin hadn't interrupted the plan, Adam would still be here today. He would be at least 6,000 years old and would be able to tell us plenty. Unfortunately, that did not happen, and we live with the reality that these bodies have become temporary vehicles and not the permanent, eternal ones God had planned for us.

Now we must take authority over sickness rather than live in a world that never knew sickness. We as Adam's offspring have lost a lot. Just how much we can regain will be explored in a later chapter.

Adam: The Perfect Ruler

What was the scope of Adam's rulership? How far reaching was it? We know that he had God's designated authority to rule creation. He was to tend the garden, name the animals, and share his life with Eve. This harmony between God and man allowed Adam to operate in full confidence. Adam's authority flowed with ease. The daily administration of his duties were not a heavy burden. I don't think that he was constantly racing back and forth stopping animal fights and keeping the rabbits out of the lettuce. How could he possibly have ruled such a vast domain in the way we normally think of rulership?

Remember who Adam was. Here was a man who had no tractor, shovel, or rake. He was naked and had no tools and still he was told to run a planet. Napoleon couldn't rule the earth even though he had the armies of France at his disposal. Adam was created by God. He was God's representative. He only had one example of authority to learn from. He learned from God. So how does God rule? God rules by the authority of His own spoken word.

> **So shall My word be that goes forth out of My mouth: it shall not return unto Me void, but it shall accomplish that**

which I please, and it shall prosper in the thing whereto I sent it.

Isaiah 55:11

It makes sense then that Adam would follow God's example, because he was made in His image and had only known authority through the spoken word of God. Adam then would have taken the authority of God's word into his heart and out of the abundance of that authority in his heart his mouth would have spoken to creation; and creation, recognizing God's authority in Adam's mouth, would have obeyed. I propose to you, therefore, that Adam ruled by the spoken word just like his Father, and nature was compelled by loving respect and cooperation to obey.

It is easy to see that if all we had to do to rule was to speak, then, in fact, one man under God could rule an entire planet. Again, we know Adam was in charge of the physical, but what was the full scope of his authority? How much was expected of him? Before we attempt to answer these questions, let's explore a few other possibilities.

Paradise Lost

In the chapters to come, we will pursue a gem of truth: What was it that Adam lost and how can the thing lost be regained? Herein lies the quest of the believers on planet earth. Everyone knows or suffers the consequences of Adam's loss. Few, however, have a clear picture of the goal of their spiritual journey. As we focus on the aim of redemption, it becomes clearer that greater understanding releases untapped power to become more eternally centered than earthly centered. This can only encourage the Church on its journey to the Kingdom coming on earth as it is in heaven.

After all, if we don't know what Adam lost (who he was before sin), then how are we to know who we are as the redeemed of the Lord after being saved from sin? Just what is our potential and how do we reach it?

Could Adam See God?

The Scriptures clearly state that Adam was with God in the cool of the evening. What was the level of their relationship? God had just created a new living thing (man). In the exchange of their relationship, how well did they know each other? Adam didn't have anyone else to talk with in the beginning except God. He had no one to learn from except God. And according to Scripture, if sin is the separation between God and man, Adam had nothing to separate him from God. If there was no sin, was there any veil between God and man? I don't think so. God had no reason to hide Himself. It was, in fact, Adam who hid from God after sin. Why would Adam hide himself from someone he had never seen? I am certain that before sin, God and man shared their lives in a wonderful, open relationship. Adam, I believe, was clothed in the beginning with the glory of God, and therefore, his nakedness wasn't an issue until after the glory departed as a result of his sin.

When the glory departed, Adam saw his nakedness as evidence of his disobedience and shame which caused him to hide from God. Our redemption includes once again being clothed with the glory of God.

> **Arise, shine; for your light is come, and the glory of the Lord is risen upon you. For, behold, the darkness shall cover the earth, and gross darkness the people: but the Lord shall arise upon you, and His glory shall be seen upon you.**
>
> **Isaiah 60:1**

How Can You Create Invisible Things?

> **For by Him were all things created, that are in heaven, and that are in earth, visible and invisible, whether they be thrones, or dominions, or principalities, or powers: all things were created by Him, and for Him.**
>
> **Collosians 1:16**

The first question to answer is: Is there anything invisible to God? The obvious answer is: No - certainly not. Then if nothing is invisible to God, why are some things invisible to us? The only reasonable conclusion is that before sin, nothing was invisible. In fact, I think a strong case could be made that, before sin, the physical and spiritual worlds coexisted. If there was no sin to separate them, Adam would have had access to both worlds.

He could see all of God's creation. When sin closed the door of access to the spiritual world, the separation of the two worlds caused the spiritual world to become invisible to mankind. The reasonable answer then is that these invisible things were not invisible to man until he lost access.

So then there are "things" that are real, visible, and tangible that exist in another dimension (the spiritual world). The fact that they cannot be seen by the physical eye does not diminish their reality but does limit our access to them.

If Adam Could See God, Could He See the Angels?

It would make sense that if there was no separation between God and man that somewhere along the way, angels might have been present. It certainly seems that Adam could see that cherubim with the flaming sword set in place by God to keep him from the tree of life.

Spiritual beings are the servants of spiritual authority. If God's rulership extends through His angelic servants, Adam may even have had angels at his disposal in his rulership of earth.

Kabash

In Genesis 1:28 God instructed Adam to take dominion over creation. The word for dominion in the Hebrew is *Kabash*. The word literally means to put your foot on the neck of your enemy and bring him under authority. This is a most interesting passage because this was before sin. Adam lived in a sin-free environment. What was there in this perfect place that needed the foot of Adam's authority? Because of the events of Genesis Chapter 2, we could reasonably conclude that Adam was to exercise authority over Satan.

Could Adam See Satan?

If Adam could see God and the angels, he would certainly be able to see Satan. If he couldn't see Satan, and God gave him authority over Satan, then how could Adam do his job? It would be extremely difficult to rule someone you couldn't see. If Satan simply had to disappear to escape Adam's authority, how then was Adam to rule? Adam's job description as God's delegated authority to rule planet earth included the *Kabash* of Satan.

Was Adam Limited to the Physical?

Is is possible that before sin there was no division between the physical and spiritual world as far as Adam was concerned? Ask yourself: Is God limited to only one dimension today? I certainly think not. The Bible clearly teaches that God has total access to all of creation.

In the same way if Adam, who had no sin, could see God, the angels, and Satan, is it also quite probable that he had access to the spiritual world? In fact, Adam may not have even known that there were two worlds.

If sin didn't separate them, what was there to divide those two worlds for him? His primary domain may have been the physical, but he could well have had spiritual access.

Where did the veil in the temple come from? Clearly, the veil was put in the temple at God's instruction to symbolize the separation that occurred because of sin. God's primary domain is the spiritual but He certainly has access to the physical. With no sin to spoil God's plan, the communion that God and man shared must have been sweet and fulfilling.

God created an entire new domain for His man Adam to rule. He intended for Adam to live forever and continually serve in the capacity for which he was created. Some believe that Adam did not have spiritual access. Then ask yourself this question: If Adam had never sinned and lived forever, would he have never seen God, heaven, or the spiritual world? If, before sin, there was no division between the physical and spiritual, I propose that Adam could well have enjoyed heaven and earth.

Heavenly Thrones

> **For we wrestle not against flesh and blood, but against principalities, against powers, against the rulers of the darkness of this world, against spiritual wickedness in high places.**
>
> **Ephesians 6:12**

Daniel refers to the Prince of Persia, a demonic ruler of the heavenlies (Daniel 10:13). This heavenly ruler hindered Gabriel the archangel when he was sent by God to deliver a message to Daniel. Colossians 1:16 refers to heavenly thrones that Christ Jesus created that are invisible. These are not thrones in heaven, but seats of authority in the heavenlies. There are unquestionable, invisible, spiritual seats of authority over planet earth. Whoever occupies these positions of rulership also enjoys the authority that accompanies the office.

Who Grants Control of These Invisible Heavenly Rulership Positions?

Obviously, it is God who sets up one and puts down another. But God is also bound by His word and covenants. The Bible calls Satan the god of this world and the prince of the power of the air. It is clear that

Satan controls some seats of authority in the heavenlies. How did he get his job? Which line did he stand in? Where did he apply? Who hired him? I think most reasonable Bible students would agree that Satan gained his present position of authority in the garden when he deceived Adam.

Adam was chosen by God to be His delegated authority but gave up that seat of authority when Satan deceived Eve (who was Adam's responsibility). All of the fellowship and extension of God's authority through man to oversee God's creation was destroyed. Man found himself separated from God.

Satan now sits in Adam's seat of authority and Adam, who was to *Kabash* (have dominion over) Satan, now found himself in the reverse position where Satan had dominion over him. God granted the office to Adam, who through sin, passed its rights and authority to another. We now find God in the awkward position of being separated legally (bound by His own words and covenants) from the one He loves.

How Far Was the Fall?

Think of man before sin. He had open fellowship with God. He enjoyed a perfect creation that was designed to thrive under man's authority. He had access to the spiritual world. He was clothed with the glory of God. He could see spiritual beings and sat on the seat of authority in the heavenlies ruling his domain with the word of God in his mouth. The physical and spiritual worlds were not separated by sin. Sounds like heaven on earth. It was. The two worlds shared a common existence.

Sin caused the physical and spiritual worlds to literally be torn apart and separated into two different dimensions. If this was *Star Trek*, we would call this a distortion of the time-space continuum. After sin, we find Adam and Eve confined to the physical world. As the judgment for Adam's sin, access to the spiritual was cut off and that world became invisible to Adam and his descendants, who were now locked in the physical world.

To see the fall in its full implication explains many things. Earth became the largest prison house in the universe. Man was locked in a physical world unable to escape back into the heavens and was now being cruelly ruled by an unseen being, Satan, who before sin, was under Adam's authority.

Adam, who previously dined on the tree of life and was clothed with the glory of God, now found himself naked and scratching the dirt for food. He was now fighting the elements for his survival and no longer had fellowship with God. I would say this scenario (Satan's usurped rulership) would certainly qualify as a fall for man.

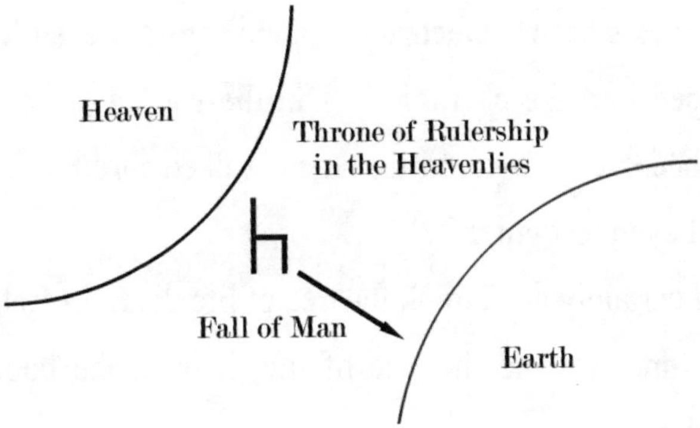

What Happened to the Tree of Life?

I know this may sound like a silly question. But we need to understand that there are reasons for everything.

Remember in Genesis 3:24 that God placed cherubim and a flaming sword at the east of the garden of Eden to guard the way to the tree of life. God didn't want Adam to have access to the tree of life any longer since he was now disqualified from his original job due to sin. If Adam had been able to eat of the tree of life after sin, mankind would have lived forever separated from the presence of God.

So what happened to the tree? If it didn't die, and the cherubim didn't desert their post, and the garden was only a physical place in the Middle East, then why in all of these years hasn't someone stumbled across the garden or bumped into the cherubim? Did the garden go to seed and become so overrun that men walked through it and didn't even recognize it?

I certainly don't think the tree of life died. In fact, the next time we find the tree of life, it is in the book of Revelation.

> **... To him who overcomes I will give to eat of the tree of life <u>which is in the midst of the paradise of God.</u>**
>
> **Revelation 2:7**

The paradise of God. The garden of God. You see, the garden of God didn't go away, but was simply separated from the physical world. Just because part of God's creation is spiritual doesn't mean that it doesn't have substance. The spiritual world exists and is just as real as the physical. In heaven there are thrones, seats, a sea of glass, the tree of life, leaves, fruit, the river of life, and the mountain of God. It is all real, but sin separated the two worlds, and one became invisible to us.

Man finds himself separated from the presence of God and from the tree of life. As bad as the problem is, the worse news is that there is nothing we can do from our side to set things right again. How can man who violated spiritual law, set things right when he finds himself restricted to a physical existence? Thank God that He loved us. If it had not been for the fact that God's love was deeper than our sin, we would have been lost forever.

Our heavenly Father's broken heart also carried a plan to help us regain what was lost. He had a plan to legally free us from our prison house and set us once again on the thrones of rulership over the earth. When His plan was complete, it would leave no exposure or future challenge to our right of rulership. He would not only set things right, but do it in a way that was right.

The quest of man since the fall has been to get back to his destiny in the heavens. Unfortunately, man has tried over and over to illegally escape the confines of earth. In Genesis Chapter 11, man attempted to build a tower that would reach into the heavens. Babel was destined to fail because it was a physical attempt to solve a spiritual problem. Had they built the tower six or seven miles high, they would have died from lack of oxygen. Space travel requires that man take an artificial atmosphere into space with him in order to survive. Even though man has physically made it off the planet, he still hasn't found his spiritual destiny and never will apart from God's plan.

Witchcraft is an attempt to solve the problem spiritually, but goes at it from the wrong side of the spiritual world. In witchcraft, man chooses to align himself with the one who presently occupies the spiritual thrones (Satan). Some small progress has been made by those who follow darkness. Astral projection, dark powers, and authority over other men have been experienced. The problem with this approach is that it is temporary and futile because the empowerer of these small, brief successes is a liar and a deceiver. Any powers granted by darkness are only intended to ensnare and entrap mankind further into a kingdom destined to fail.

Yes, we are of Adam's seed and our destiny is the heavens, but to qualify, we must trust the plan of God who loves us and who wants to legally restore us to our rightful place. The depth and wisdom of the plan, we hope to unfold in the following chapters.

Chapter III

Putting the Pieces Together

Wouldn't life be simpler if God would just come right out and tell us what to do, what He meant, and what was going to happen? For many people, the Scriptures speak in circles, stories, and symbols that disguise the wisdom we seek. Man has struggled to decipher the hidden mysteries of prophecy throughout the centuries.

Even after three years of daily ministry with the disciples, Jesus told them in **John 16:12,**

> **I have yet many things to say unto you, but you cannot bear them <u>now</u>.**

Does that mean that we might be able to bear them later? From the next verse in **John 16:13**, we have some hope. Not only will the Holy Spirit guide us to truth, but He will show us things to come.

> **Howbeit when He, the Spirit of truth, is come, He will guide you into all truth: for He shall not speak of Himself; but whatsoever He shall hear, that shall He speak: and He will show you things to come.**

God has always had a way of saying things that makes man scratch his head to figure out what He really said. He said He speaks in mysteries so that only the children of the Kingdom might have the truth. The Holy Spirit was sent to guide us into truth. Apparently, there are two factors that determine the unfolding of God's mysteries. First our hunger, openness, desire, previous understanding, etc. determine how God wonderfully and individually unfolds His marvelous secrets to each believer. Second is His timing. Have you ever picked up a book that has been lying around the house for years? You may have tried to read it four or five times before, but this time the words suddenly come alive. Thrill of thrills, you have been led to a new truth; your excitement cries out to share it with a friend. You try your best to share your excitement, but your friend simply cannot understand why you're so excited. It is as if God has customized a spiritual curriculum for each of us to mature us into a finished product of His pleasing. That is why we are admonished not to be preoccupied with comparing ourselves with others.

With this kind of divine schooling, the only true standard becomes, "How are you doing with God's plan for **your** life?" If I begin comparing myself with God's plan for somebody else's life, I will become confused and spiritually disoriented and ultimately guilt ridden. How could I ever live up to God's plan for somebody else?

When some **new** truth settles into our inner man, was it really that the truth was new or that it was simply new to us? Obviously, the truth was true before we understood it. It is just new to us. The body of truth in the Scriptures is there for all believers. In practical experience, however, we appropriate that truth at different times and paces. The process of adding new truth to our internal belief system is called growth. Hopefully, this process will continue throughout our lives, and we will never stop asking questions and growing from the answers we find.

Show Us Things to Come

Thank God for the divine work of the Holy Spirit in our lives. He comforts and teaches us about our daily walk as believers. Most believers understand "the guiding us into truth" part. We have all had our own little "Ah ha!"- breakthroughs in growth. But there is more to this life than knowing the rules of the Kingdom. We must fellowship with the vision of God for our generation. I believe in our time, as never before, God desires to share His eternal viewpoint with the Church. The Holy Spirit is also available to show us things to come.

Why do we need to concern ourselves with future events? In order to pay the price required of us in the days to come, we need to see the reward. Jesus *for the joy that was set before Him endured the cross, despising the shame* (Heb12:2). Jesus' understanding of future events helped Him pay the price. His long range planning for the redeemed must make sense concerning some dark days that lie just ahead. Keep reminding yourself as you read on that God has a plan and it will work.

When the eyes of Elisha's servant were opened and he saw the warriors of heaven ready to fight the enemy for them, his confidence level shot up and his fear melted away. I pray that your personal moment of enlightenment comes to the point that your confidence stands up strong in these days. Divine understanding will help you become a fearless soldier of the Kingdom through revelation knowledge. Seeing the days ahead through God's eyes with God's understanding will strengthen the resolve of those who are to be involved in these coming events.

Before we attempt to unfold what we believe to be revelation knowledge, there are some basics that we must review in order to lay the proper foundation to build on. As we understand fully the events which are to unfold, we too, once we lose our fear, can then become willing to pay the price expected of us in the days to come. God has always used symbols to deliver His best secrets. He used a lamb being slaughtered in Isaiah 53 to tell of Jesus' sacrifice. He used a dove to tell of the Holy Spirit's power coming on Jesus' life. He used an olive tree to instruct Israel, and so on. Our journey to understanding this proper foundation for revelation knowledge begins in Daniel.

Most present and past teachers of prophetic understanding begin with Daniel's revelations and visions. The reason is quite simple. Here we find one of the few symbolic passages in Scripture that is immediately followed by the divine explanation. Let's examine Daniel's vision of the four beasts.

Chapter IV

Daniel's Four Beasts

In Daniel, some basics for understanding "things to come" are laid down for us to build on. Daniel's deep love for his people led him to a prayer relationship with God, thus living a life of spiritual example to Babylon. His concern for Israel's deliverance compelled him to search in the heavenlies for answers.

One day, while prospecting heaven in prayer, God wonderfully unfolded some of eternity's secrets in a vision. Daniel saw four beasts. You might well imagine how you would feel in a similar situation. You prayed for something and God showed you four weird looking animals. Without the meaning, you would be left totally confused. The mystery would remain a mystery. But here God very specifically unfolds the meaning of future events.

The following are the beasts which Daniel saw:

Beast #1 - Daniel 7:4 - A lion with eagle's wings

Beast #2 - Daniel 7:5 - A bear raised up on one side

with three ribs in its mouth

Beast #3 - Daniel 7:6 - A leopard with four heads and four wings

Beast #4 - Daniel 7:7 - A dreadful beast with 10 horns and iron teeth

After Daniel saw this great sight, his response was much like ours may have been:

> **I Daniel was grieved in my spirit in the midst of my body and the visions of my head troubled me.**
>
> **Daniel 7:15**

Revelation knowledge is a double-edged sword. Everybody wants to know what is coming, but what is revealed to you may not be so exciting. In Revelation, John wrote that it was sweet to his mouth, but bitter to his belly. Daniel was troubled to say the least. He asked one of the (angels) standing nearby to help him know what the vision he saw meant.

Daniel was told that the four beasts represented four kings or kingdoms which shall rise out of the earth. With the explanation that follows (Read Dan. 7:10-28) taken with Dan. 2 and Dan. 8, the following becomes quite clear:

Beast #1 is Babylon.

Beast #2 is the Medo-Persian Empire.

Beast #3 is the Grecian Empire ruled by Alexander the Great.

Beast #4 is the Roman Empire which will rise again in the last days.

Without writing an entire book on Daniel's visions, let's draw one piece of information to use later. God used beasts as symbols to tell Daniel about the course of human history from an earthly prospective. He warned that these beasts would *come up from the se*a (Dan. 7:3) and *...arise out of the earth* (Dan. 7:17). Daniel's visions would chronicle the changes of world governments.

How does the world change governments? What is the vehicle by which power transitions from one group to another? Throughout history, change has not come easily. We call these transitions **War!** (The concept of transition will be discussed in more detail in a later chapter.) When Babylon lost its dominant role in world events, there was war. The Medo-Persian Empire conquered Babylon. Blood flowed like water when nations competed for control. History books are the stories of the rise and fall of nations. The Medo-Persians were conquered by the Grecians, and the Grecians were conquered by the Romans. There have been wars and rumors of wars ever since.

Among Christian scholars, there is little debate as to the meaning of Daniel's visions because the interpretations are clearly spelled out right in the text. The real challenge comes when God gives visions and does not immediately give a clear cut explanation of the meaning. Spiritual thinkers are left to guess at the meaning, and mankind almost always guesses wrong. The divisions begin and groups gather around those who are the most persuasive with their guesses.

Man is always wanting to make sense out of things he doesn't understand. The truth is that until a secret is revealed, you can guess all you want and you still won't know for sure.

Chapter V

Secrets Revealed--Secrets Concealed

Even though God has graciously shown man much of His heart and His plan, there is certainly much yet to be discovered. Throughout time, as God has revealed truths, there have been major shakeups on earth. The law of Israel propelled them to material, physical, and spiritual prominence in the natural world. Jesus' ministry, with the ability to change the heart (belief system) of man, has transplanted the heart of God into a brutal world. Mankind is forever changed because Jesus came.

The question remains: Has God revealed all He will reveal before Jesus' return? There are some clues found in Scripture. In the midst of Daniel's abundance of revelations, God showed him many things to come. But in Dan. 8:26, God says something quite unusual. God told Daniel to *...shut you up the vision; for it shall be for many days.* In Rev. 10:4, when the seven thunders uttered their voices and John was about to write down what he heard, a voice from heaven said, *Seal up those things which the seven thunders uttered and write them* *not*. In 1 Cor 2:9-10, Paul quotes Isaiah 64:4 and says that God is revealing things to His Church by the Holy Spirit. Referring back again to John 16:12, certainly at some point in time, the Church should receive the information that Jesus wants to reveal.

Could it be true that God has yet more mysteries to reveal to a hungry church? Many believers are crying out, "Is this all there is?" Despite all of our meetings, money, and missions, we are not winning the war for the souls of men. Could God have some fresh information--a different approach that would increase our effectiveness? Is it time for a new wineskin for the ministry of the last days?

Many times in our Christian growth, the key to unlock new understanding and power is simply seeing situations from a different perspective. In the chapters to follow, we shall attempt to look at some old information from a different vantage point. Whatever secrets God has been holding for the last days will have as profound an effect on the Church and humanity as the Law and the ministry of Jesus had on those who preceded us.

Earth Reflects Heaven

Which came first: earth or heaven? This little trip may seem on the surface a bit silly, but the answer to this question is quite necessary. Bear with me for a few minutes.

Heaven was certainly around before earth, and the Scriptures tell us that the things on earth are only patterns or a reflection of the true which are in heaven. If you think there are beautiful spots on earth, wait until you see heaven. Heaven has trees, mountains, rivers, fruit, streets, mansions, seats, clean air, horses, and so on.

Earth has these things because heaven had them first and earth reflects heaven. Even man was made in the image and likeness of God. Hebrews 9:23-24 clearly says that if the earthly patterns of heavenly worship needed to be cleansed by blood, then the true heavenly center of worship needed to have Jesus' blood presented there to deal with man's sin permanently.

Moses was told to build the earthly worship center after the pattern that was given to him on the mountain. The heavenly temple has a holiest place and an altar and so did Moses' temple. All of these heavenly things sit on something besides clouds. Heaven is a real place with substance to support all that the Scriptures tell us is there.

Could there be other similarities? Why has man always tried to elevate man in leadership positions? Heaven has a Ruler and so man wants one, but not always the same One heaven has. Man has tried to make heaven on earth without the heart of heaven. Man will always fail until he submits and heaven rules earth through men.

Which brings us back to Daniel's beasts. These four beasts give us a brief record of human history with a glimpse of heavenly history. While Nebuchadnezzar and Babylon start as the lion and are overcome by the Bear of the Medes and Persians (earthly history), Daniel hears from an angel. Gabriel tells Daniel that he was detained for 21 days by the Prince of Persia (heavenly history). This was obviously a ruler of darkness influencing the affairs of earthly kingdoms. The Persians eventually did prevail against the Babylonians.

If we could see the unseen world and record heavenly events, wouldn't it be interesting to read that history book. After all, from what we have seen in the previous paragraphs, what was happening here was only a reflection of what was happening there. If we only had that book to read. Maybe men could have that slightly different perspective needed to gain the understanding of the mysteries of the last days. Maybe God did leave us a time capsule of heavenly history in an obscure passage in Revelation.

Chapter VI

The Four Beasts of Heaven

And before the throne there was a sea of glass like unto crystal; and in the midst of the throne, and round about the throne, were four beasts full of eyes before and behind. And the first beast was like a lion, and the second beast like a calf, and the third beast had a face as a man, and the fourth beast was like a flying eagle. And the four beasts had each of them six wings about him; and they were full of eyes within; and they rest not day and night, saying, "Holy, holy, holy, Lord God Almighty, which was, and is, and is to come."

Revelation 4:6

If we are to learn anything from prophetic symbolism, we must see that there are reasons for the things that are recorded. If the books of the world could not hold all that Jesus did, then certainly what was given to us in Scripture must have some importance.

If the four beasts of Daniel represented four different eras of human government on a physical level, could it be that the four beasts of heaven represented some sequence or time frames or period of God's dealing with mankind from a heavenly perspective?

God is concerned about far more than simply tracking historical events. After the fall of man, God set out immediately to put into motion a plan to redeem and restore man. The four beasts of Revelation not only tell of history from a heavenly vantage point, but also reveal a progressive plan to redeem and restore to man what was lost in the garden. From the fall to final judgment, God has been working and will continue to work with man to restore that which was lost. To accomplish His goals, from time to time, new rules have been put in place in order to nurse man back to spiritual health. God's goal has always been to see us restored to a position to fulfill His plan for us. To do that we must regain what Adam lost.

There was a time when God and man shared regularly in a face to face fellowship. Adam, as God's representative, ruled planet earth. Both the physical and spiritual history of man could have been recorded in a single book until sin separated the two worlds. Adam sinned; man fell and separation occurred. We pick up human history with the fall of man. As heaven records God's perspective of human events, the first beast is revealed.

Chapter VII

Beast #1--The Lion

Due to sin, Adam, who before knew only peace and the flow of God's authority, was locked on planet earth in a life and death struggle to survive. Nature, which previously was under Adam's authority and cooperated with him as God's man, was now his enemy and worked against him. Adam had to fight the elements, insects, beasts, and almost everything just to survive. Now it was by the sweat of his brow, not by the authority of his words, that he survived.

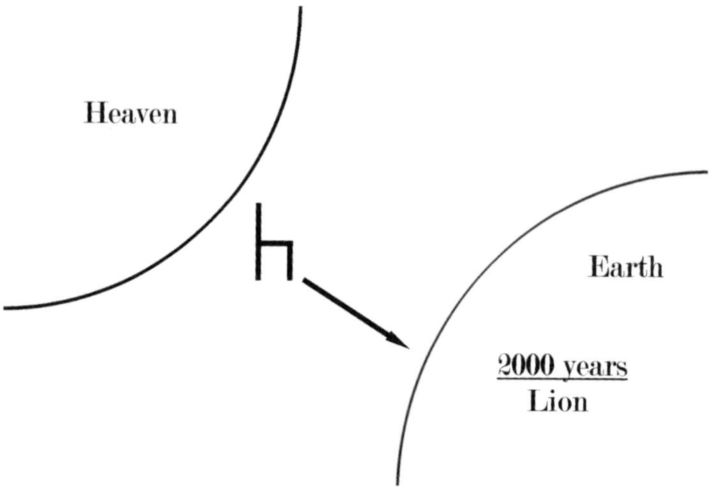

As the human family on earth grew, there was no clear cut law or rule to dictate the course of human history. When conflicts arose, the only way man had to resolve conflicts was through his physical strength. The strongest prevailed and imposed his wishes on those he conquered. There was no defender of the weak or anyone to mediate conflicts.

In Gen. 10:8-9, Nimrod was said to have hunted men as others hunted animals, and there was no law to stop him. In Gen. 14:14, Abram heard that his nephew Lot had been captured when Sodom and Gomorah had been plundered. He took 318 trained servants from his own house and defeated the five kings of the North who were holding Lot. In fact, when he returned from battle, his victory began to build a reputation. In those days respect came from strength. Abimilech wanted to make a peace covenant with Abraham because Abraham was a great warrior and as a result had great wealth. Fear led weaker men to seek peace with stronger men.

Over and over we see early human history as a story of the strong doing what he pleased and the weak watching from the shadows. The lion certainly was a good selection to symbolize this first period of man's history. The lion was king of the jungle where the rule was survival of the fittest. Life was simple. Every man did what was right in his own eyes. For many, many years there was no one to tell him any differently. God dealt with man through his conscience. Social order was enforced by the strength of men's arms.

The period lasted approximately 2,000 years. As the Age of the Lion begins to draw to a close, we see Abraham's family (now somewhere between two to six million people) in captivity being ruled by the strong arm of Egypt. Over a period of 430 years, while Israel was in Egypt, the Israelites grew greatly in number. In fact, there were so many Israelites that the Egyptians began to fear them (Exodus 1:7-14). To keep Israel under control, the Egyptians slowly began to restrict their freedoms. The end result of Egypt's fear was Israel's bondage. Israel became a nation of slaves to the stronger Lion of Egypt. (The Sphinx of Egypt looked very much like the lion.)

As the years mounted, Israel's oppression caused them to cry out to God for deliverance. When God took notice of the cry of His people, Moses was chosen to lead them out of Egypt and into the "Promised Land." He was also going to lead them out of one age and into another.

And the Lord said, I have surely seen the affliction of My people who are in Egypt, and have heard their cry by reason of their taskmasters; for I know their sorrows; And I am come down to deliver them out of the hand of the Egyptians, and to bring them up out of that land unto a good land and a large, unto a land flowing with milk and honey; unto the place of the Canaanites, and the Hittites, and the Amorites, and the Perizzites, and the Hivites, and the Jebusites. Now therefore, behold, the cry of the children of Israel is come unto Me and I have also seen the oppression wherewith the Egyptians oppress them. Come now therefore, and I will send you unto Pharaoh, that you may bring forth My people the children of Israel out of Egypt.

Exodus 3:7-10

To more fully understand these time periods or ages and how mankind moved from one age to another, we should answer a few questions:

1. Why was it necessary for things to change?

God loves man so much that He has set out on a plan to restore the descendants of Adam to their rightful place of rulership. Since God is a God of order, decency, and righteousness, He had to institute a plan of redemption or restoration that would regain a right relationship for man. This plan would have to be one that could not be contested by Satan who was not intended to be the god of this world. Under the law of the jungle, man would never regain his loss. It is impossible for the arm of the flesh to solve the problem. Through series or sequences of God arranged seasons, man would gradually awaken to greater and greater understanding of his destiny.

Israel was in bondage in Egypt making bricks without straw. The people of destiny had totally lost sight of the greatness of God's plan. Sometimes circumstances will motivate us to move to another place. Israel finally became so uncomfortable with their present situation that they were willing to listen to Moses when he presented the option of leaving Egypt for some distant Promised Land. Elijah was motivated to move when the brook dried up. The lepers at the gate moved outside the city because they were hungry. When people become uncomfortable enough with the status quo, they will move. Sometimes circumstances can provide good incentive for change. God was ready to move Israel to the next level of understanding toward His goal of full redemption.

2. Who Initiated the Change?

The burdens that Egypt placed on Israel eventually became unbearable. While their work quotas increased, their supplies decreased and their taskmasters ruled them with cruelty. Tell me, if you were working in the brick pits of Egypt and one day your straw was taken away, what would you pray for that night? Most of us would not have the insight to say, "God is just strengthening my resolve to finally be delivered from Egypt." Most of us would have prayed for straw. Often when God is arranging events to bless us in the long run, it gets uncomfortable in the short run. God's goal was to deliver Israel into a land flowing with milk and honey, not to simply solve their straw problem.

When you find yourself hungering for God's deliverance, don't be surprised if things take a turn for the worse. Always keep this in mind: God does love you and has a plan for your life. When things get uncomfortable, resist the temptation to ask for straw. Rather, ask for wisdom to see what God is up to. He may be working on something exceeding abundantly above what you could ask or think.

And the LORD said, I have surely seen the affliction of my people which are in Egypt, and have heard their cry by reason of their taskmasters; for I know their sorrows;

Exodus 3:7

The people began to cry out for deliverance. As so often is the case, God moves in response to the cries of His people. The cries of Israel were a clear indication that they were now willing to entertain the idea that maybe there was something better for them than Egypt. If God sends deliverance before we are willing to accept it as an option, then we may not move. Circumstance often softens our will to accept a different viewpoint.

3. Who was the Agent of Change?

The answer to this question will become increasingly more important as we move to the later ages. The good news and bad news is that God works through men. It's good news to us when God uses us for His great and mighty works. It's not always good news when we first hear what God is up to. Many times His plans are truly greater than ours. Often we find ourselves struggling to embrace where God is heading and how He wants to use us to get there. In this case we find that God, in response to Israel crying out for help, confronted Moses with the problem. When God spoke through the burning bush and explained Israel's need for help, Moses agreed that something should be done. But when God told Moses that he was the chosen one to lead Israel out of Egypt to the Promised Land, suddenly Moses saw things differently.

Moses argued, "But God, I'm 80 years old and wanted for murder in Egypt. You know the Egyptians and the Jews have a dislike for me. Besides, I can't speak clearly; they won't listen to me. Who am I to pull this off anyway?"

Many times throughout history God has tapped the shoulder of an agent of change. Gideon, Daniel, David, Saul, and many others have felt the greatness of God's plan confronting the weakness of their own abilities. Listen to the account of God talking to Moses:

> **And Moses said unto God, Who am I, that I should go unto Pharaoh, and that I should bring forth the children of Israel out of Egypt?**
>
> **And He said, Certainly I will be with you; and this shall be a token unto you, that I have sent you.**
>
> **Exodus 3:11-12**

To be a God anointed agent of change requires that we trust completely in that divine "Certainly, I will be with you."

Summary of the Age of the Lion

After man's first 2,000 years of history, God was ready for a change. Man was being called to a higher level. The law of the jungle was now to be replaced by a better system. Circumstances prepared the people to receive the change, and their discomfort with the old system caused them to call to heaven for change. In response to the cry of the people, God sent Moses--the agent of change--to take them through a period of transition to the next step in God's progressive redemptive plan.

Key Elements of the Age of the Lion

1. Length of Age - 2,000 years from the fall to the giving of the Law
2. Rule of Age - Survival of the fittest
3. Motivation of Transition - Israel's discontentment with their present situation, making the thought of moving easier
4. Agent of Change - Moses, God's chosen one to lead Israel out of Egypt (where the stronger ruled) into the Promised Land
5. Length of Transition - 40 years in the wilderness

Each new dispensation of God's dealing with man brings with it a new set of rules. The rule of the day with the Lion was that the strongest survived and ruled the weaker. Now that the Lion was finished, God's progressive plan of redemption for His people was about to take a giant step forward. For the first time since Adam's fall, earth was going to have a structure for human culture that was given by heaven. Man would no longer do what was right in his own eyes, but now would do what was right according to a heaven-authored code of conduct for the Jewish nation. When Moses was up on the mountain for the season of fasting and fellowship with God, the Law was given by God Himself and the age of the second heavenly beast was established.

Chapter VIII

Beast #2--The Calf

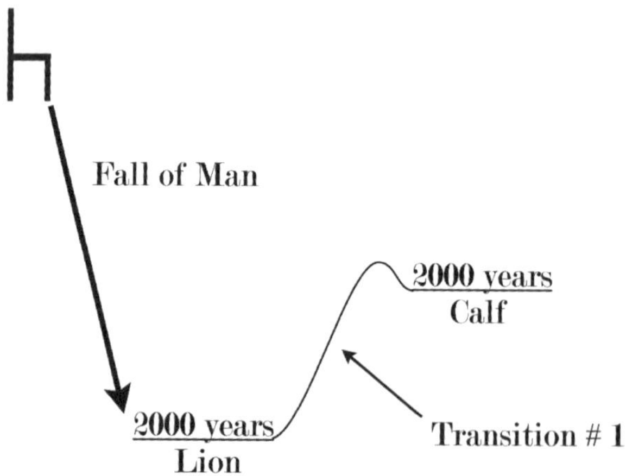

This new beginning was a wonderful time for Israel. God had visited man and left behind a code of conduct (the Law of Moses) for man to live by. Everywhere Israel turned, the favor of God was on them. Their nation prospered in the new land and they saw victory after victory over their enemies. The Law gave them security and order under this new code of conduct called "The Law of Moses." The weak now had a defender. The widow now had an advocate. Even the offender now had a way to rectify his wrongs.

For most offenses under the Law, there was provision by sacrifice to deal with the offense. The calf (the second beast of Revelation) became the symbol of forgiveness by sacrifice for sins and was an appropriate symbol for the Age of the Law. Even though these sacrifices could not wipe away sin, they did provide a covering for sin. They could not impart eternal life, but they at least provided a way of instituting some social justice. Man began to take notice of his conscience and attempted to come to grips with his guilt. The inner man still yearned for eternal forgiveness. The Law brought him face to face with the harsh reality that he needed more than a covering for his sins. God's progressive plan of redemption would eventually bring man what he needed.

This era began with a strange event. As the Law was being given, which would improve man's condition, the enemy of man put it into the heart of the people to build a golden calf to worship. This was an attempt to miscarriage the Law by eliminating Israel through the worship of a false god, a calf, the very creature God appointed to become a blood sacrifice for their sins. Just remember, when everything is done by the vote of the majority and the will of the people, mankind will usually get itself into real trouble. The people pressed Aaron to build a god to worship. America should take a lesson from this event. America has, as a majority, voted itself many golden calves.

In the early days of the Lion, Satan attempted through his Tower of Babel and the race of the giants to shortcut God's plan. Abraham emerged as bold as a lion to be God's man and birth a nation. In the last days of the Lion, the strength of Egypt tried to stamp out the people of God. In the end, the people of God prevailed by the grace and miracles of God.

In the early days of the calf, again there was an attempt to discredit and derail the next step of God's redemption. The Law was, however, firmly put into place and the result was a 2,000 year age where God's primary dealing with mankind was through the Jewish nation.

As the Age of the Calf was drawing to a close, once again the people of God found themselves in bondage. Just before the next age arrived, the Law had been interpreted and reinterpreted to the point that nobody could keep the Law with all of its explanations and extensions. They found themselves not in bondage to the taskmasters of Egypt but to the confines of the very Law they loved so much. They were no longer making physical bricks without straw but were now in servitude to an imperfect system that had lost its joy. They still appeared at the synagogues, but the thrill was gone. Israel was not only in bondage to the Romans, but in greater bondage to their own traditions.

Jesus said in Matt 15:6b *...Thus have you made the commandment of God of none effect by your tradition.* Their deep discontentment with their present circumstances once again opened the door for change. This time the cry of Israel for a deliverer caused a different response from heaven. When God heard the cry for deliverance, He sent Jesus (Agent of Change) to free them from the bondage in their hearts, not to free them from the physical bondage and tyranny of Rome. While Israel was looking for physical deliverance, God once again had planned something better.

Was the Law (Calf) Better Than the Age of the Conscience (Lion)?

If you would have asked Israel under the Law if they wanted to go back to the old way of the Lion, they would have laughed. The benefits of the Law were miles ahead of the time preceding the Law. Yet, even with all the benefits the Law brought to Israel, the emptiness of their heart wasn't satisfied. Man still needed more revelation from God to complete his journey to full redemption.

Thanks be to God who heard the cry of His people and sent them what they needed and not what they asked for. If God had only destroyed the Romans and not torn down their traditions, they would have been in the same eternal, hopeless place of need. It was fully time for the age of the third beast.

Summary of the Age of the Calf

While this age was by no means the end of the journey, it certainly was a step in the right direction toward the restoration back to the place from which man had fallen. God's blessing on the nation made them the envy of their neighbors. But this was only a step. The Law of Moses could never bring the full restoration of man. More was needed.

Key Elements of the Age of the Calf

1. Length of the Age - 2,000 years from the giving of

the Law to the resurrection of Christ and the coming of the Holy Spirit to the Church

2. Rule of the Age - The Law of Moses
3. Motivation of Transition - The Law becoming so burdensome that no one was able to comply with all its rules
4. Agent of Change - Jesus, sent by the Father to seek and to save that which was lost
5. Length of Transition - Jesus' life of 33 years including His death and resurrection and fulfilling of the Law.

Chapter IX

Beast # 3--Man

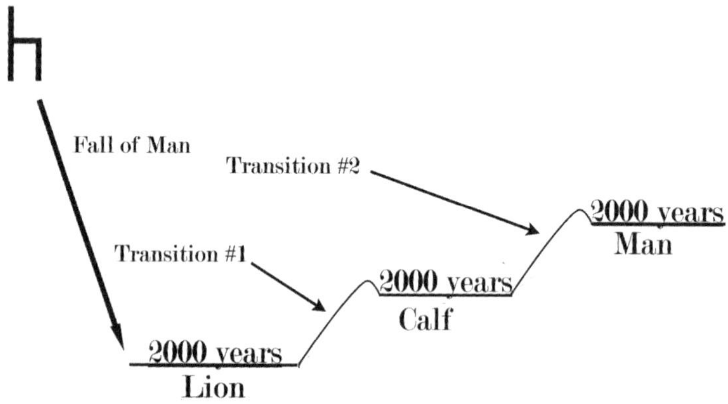

There can be no mistake about the age that followed the Law. The Scriptures say that in the fullness of time the Father sent His only begotten Son to seek and to save that which was lost. Let's answer some questions about several points raised in earlier chapters.

1. What was attempted to discredit God's plan?

First, God's plan was to send His own Son (God and man in one) in human flesh to die for the sins of the world. By the time Jesus arrived on planet earth, the concept of a man being God was not a new thing. The

Roman Empire taught all of its citizens that Caesar was a god. He was worshipped as God.

This, in fact, was the crux of the argument the Jewish leaders used to manipulate Pilot to crucify Jesus. They blackmailed Pilot by saying if you don't kill this man who claims to be God, we will tell Caesar that you are not keeping the law of the Roman government that recognizes only Caesar as God. By threatening to take away Pilot's job security, they were able to manipulate him to consent to having Jesus killed.

When Jesus was born with the promise of being king of the Jews, it was King Herod's job security that was on the line, and he had all the babies in Judea killed trying to stop this new Age of the Son of Man. The Jewish leadership tried to kill Jesus several times before they actually succeeded because their positions were threatened. To our benefit, all attempts to discredit and derail Jesus' mission failed. He accomplished all He was sent to do and the time of the third beast of heaven began right on time.

2. How did God plan to take His people to a new level of understanding?

Remember that the Age of the Calf was better than the Age of the Lion, so the Age of Man should be better than the Age of the Calf. In the Gospels and in Hebrews, we find this very issue dissected and discussed at great lengths. For nearly 2,000 years the Age of the Calf sought obedience to laws written in stone. God replaced an old order that could never be lived up to with a new order that would write the desires, plans, and nature of our heavenly Father on the fleshy tablets of our hearts.

When Israel came to the conclusion that they couldn't keep the Law perfectly, they were grateful for the covering of the blood of the calf. Now God was saying that His Son's sacrifice would not only deal with the effects of sin, but the cause of sin (Romans 5-6). If you get to know Him and live in Him, you can cease from your own works, rest in Him, and be done with sin.

Imagine what a radical message that was to a nation which was heavily works oriented. In fact, the Law demanded a works mentality. The new message was now a belief mentality. The works would now flow out of a changed heart that wanted to do good things. Mankind no longer had only a written code of conduct given by God on the mountain. We now had the possibility of God actually moving inside our spirit man and by covenant forming a working partnership to press forward God's agenda for the human race.

Romans 8 says that all of creation groans and travails waiting for the manifestation of the sons of God.

> **For the earnest expectation of the creature waits for the manifestation of the sons of God.**
>
> **Romans 8:19**

> **For we know that the whole creation groans and travails in pain together until now.**
>
> **Romans 8:22**

This meant that those who approach God in the Third Age will come by faith, be made clean by Jesus' blood, and be sent into the world just like Jesus was sent. Boy is that different than going to the temple on Saturday, killing a turtle dove or a sheep or a calf to cover your sins? Now by the blood of Jesus and faith in Him both sins and the guilt of sins were washed away.

Blotting out the handwriting of ordinances that was against us, which was contrary to us, and took it out of the way, nailing it to His cross.

Colossians 2:14

What a glorious transformation from the Age of the Calf to the Age of Man! Ask anyone who lived under the Law and then found grace, if they would like to forget grace and go back to the confines of the Law. Anyone who has truly tasted the goodness of God and the mercy of forgiveness of sins would think it insane to want to go back to the Law with its ritual and incompleteness. So if this era is so wonderful, what could possibly happen toward the end of this age that would cause the people of God to come under bondage to the point that they would begin to cry out to God for deliverance?

Remember that in the Age of the Calf, the same Law that once set Israel apart and blessed them, later bound them. In the beginning, God visited the tabernacle and temple with His glory. The communion level between God and His people was very high and close. But by the end of the Age of the Calf, all that Israel had left was a traditional, ceremonial remembrance of the glory they once shared as a nation with God. All of the same holy days were observed. The people still tithed and prayed the same prayers. But despite the fact that everything looked the same, something had changed. Something was missing. It seemed as if Israel was still showing up on the Sabbath, but God wasn't.

In Isaiah, God said that He had had enough of their sacrifices because Israel's heart was no longer in their worship. Paraphrased, God said to them, "Since you have drifted away from Me in your heart, I really am not enjoying this anymore." The glory faded, and once God stopped going to church, the people weren't happy going anymore either.

Emptiness was the rule of the day. Since nobody wanted to have God upset with them, they kept their traditions, even though they no longer meant anything. It was into this emptiness in the hearts of men that Jesus came. It was the discontentment with the old way of doing things that drew a heavenly response.

So what about the end of the age of the third heavenly beast--the Age of the Son of Man? This age certainly began with great joy and excitement. The day the Church was born, all of Jerusalem knew something wonderful had occurred. The glory of God had once again returned to Israel and soon began to spread to the Gentiles. The people of God once again marveled in the clouds of God's glory. Miracles were daily occurrences. Thousands upon thousands of people were flocking to the Shepherd and Bishop of their souls. Heaven and earth were once again in touch.

> **God also bearing them witness, both with signs and wonders, and with divers miracles, and gifts of the Holy Ghost, according to His own will.**
>
> **Hebrews 2:4**

Is it possible in our day, at the end of the Age of the Third Beast, that we the Church are experiencing the same thing that happened to Israel? Could what was delivered to us in purity now be so twisted by tradition that we are left with empty traditions that have worn God out? Could He be saying to us, "I've had enough of your empty worship!"? If this is true, it is both good news and bad news for the people of God.

This bittersweet knowledge tells us that great emptiness and discontentment will sweep through the Kingdom. For many believers, the joy of going to church isn't the same as it once was. We will have problems with the leadership of the church as they desperately try to keep the old order intact. This was the mistake of the leadership of the Jewish nation at the end of the Age of the Calf. God was moving on to His next phase of redemption and those who led the old order wanted to stay in the security of the old: the empty, dead, but predictable way of doing things.

People resist change even when it is good for them. If we resist too strongly, we may just become a casualty of the new. The good news is something new and better is coming. For the hungry, seeking, true believers who are calling out for deliverance from the bondage of empty tradition, God is once again about to make His move. Already the sign of new things is sprouting as a new crop just breaking the soil. Conversely, the false (such as the New Age Movement and many others) is beginning to appear in an attempt to discredit and diminish what God is about to do in response to the present level of holy discontentment. His progressive, redemptive plan is once again about to birth fresh revelation that will propel true worshippers into a totally new dimension of kingdom living.

Summary of the Age of the Son of Man

Jesus' life, death, and resurrection brought hope to mankind that heaven was reaching to man to solve his problem of separation from God created by sin. Now that man had a way to deal with the wages of sin, a personal relationship with God was possible once again. As man explores these new possibilities, his growth in spiritual understanding leads to a desire to see Christ's return and the Millennium begin.

Key Elements of the Age of the Son of Man

1. Length of Age - Approximately 2,000 years from the birth of the Church in Acts 2 until the present
2. Rule of Age - Law of God written in our hearts
3. Motivation of Transition - The lack of fresh vision and life in the status quo of the established church along with a desire to see Satan bound for 1,000 years
4. Agent of Change - The sons of God (to be discussed in a later chapter)
5. Length of Transition - Seven years: The Great Tribulation to the world; the greatest opportunity in history for the Church

Chapter X

Transition #1

Before we venture into the Age of the Eagle (Beast #4), there is one important piece of the puzzle that must be looked at closely. In order to get from one place to another, changes must take place. It is impossible to be in someplace new and stay in someplace old at the same time. When it was time for Abraham to inherit the Promised Land, God spoke to him and told him to leave where he was and go to a new place. If he had not left the old behind, the new would never have been found.

Change is one of the biggest challenges in life. All of us are constantly changing. We are all continually journeying from one place in life to another. We begin as a five to ten pound bundle of flesh and blood that can do nothing for ourselves. Growth and maturity to independence and adulthood require literally hundreds of changes. Most of them for that brief period are painful, awkward, and even embarrassing. We fear what we don't know; and if we are not determined to go on, we could miss some of life's most rewarding experiences. Maturity is facing the challenge of change, taking a deep breath, and pressing on to the new.

Do you remember:

your first try at riding a bicycle?

your first roller skates?

the seventh grade?

standing on the high diving board for the first time?

your first solo drive in the family car?

your first traffic ticket?

your first date?

your first airplane flight?

your first day on a real job?

buying your first car?

walking the aisle to be married?

having your first baby?

leading your first convert to Christ?

buying your first home?

All these changes are part of life. If you stop short of living *through* life's experiences, life becomes full of *what ifs* or *I wish I'ds* or *if onlys*. Usually people who face life's challenges and go on are happier and better adjusted for future adversities or changes than those who don't. Very seldom do you hear someone say, "I wish I'd never learned to ride a bike." Learning to ride a bike is challenging at the moment, but once you learn how, it is something you never forget for the rest of your life.

In God's master plan for mankind, there were some similar challenges. To move mankind from the Age of the Lion (survival of the fittest) to the Age of the Calf (the Law), God had to effect some major changes. As the conditions deteriorated in Egypt, God held out a carrot on the end of the stick. The Promised Land flowing with milk and honey was waiting on the other side of the transition from one age to the next. To move, the saints must deal with their fears. Fear of the unknown must be overcome by the excitement of new things. The clearer we see the future (the land flowing with milk and honey), the less we fear the change.

So how do you get two million Israelites, who have never lived any place but Egypt, to move to a new place which they have never seen on the other side of a desert wilderness? To coax them out of one place into another, God began His own wonderful way of encouragement. The discomfort of staying in Egypt increased and increased much like a woman in travail until the thought of leaving for a new place didn't seem so bad.

God's personal involvement in this delicate time of change is quite curious. Never before in human history do we see such personal attention from heaven as was given to Israel in getting them out of Egypt and into Canaan--out of lawlessness into the Law. As the move began, God turned up the display of His power and presence as never before. He didn't back away until the transition was complete.

Transition #1

The surge in the display of God's power on behalf of His people is unmistakable. Sure heaven had touched man before, but never before in such a dynamic way as for a whole nation to make a 40 year journey and arrive at the destination a totally new people. The transition was just as important as what preceded and what followed.

Israel was delivered by God not only out of Egypt, but into Canaan. He held their hand the whole way and demonstrated His presence through the pillar of fire, the cloud, the manna, etc. The Israel that left Egypt for the change ahead left full of fear, anxiety, and excitement all rolled together.

Much like we face our changes, they faced theirs. When they arrived in the Promised Land, however, they were a wilderness-hardened and a God-confident people. The transition worked such wonders that the fear of them was all over their enemies. Did the change do them good? Once they had tasted this new freedom from Egypt, the favor of God in battle, and the order and blessing of the Law, the transition was forever complete.

But what about the whining in the wilderness and the desire to return to Egypt? Remember we said that change wasn't always easy; but if it is God's change, it will work out for the best. Many times when we struggle with putting on the new, the newness seems impossible to get comfortable with at first.

When you first learn to drive, it doesn't come naturally; the movements are jerky and it seems we will forever drive looking at the road just 10 feet in front of the car. This discomfort makes it appear that the ease of the new will never come. Will we ever feel comfortable again? That is what Israel was facing. Will we ever again feel the predictability we once knew in Egypt?

When the heat is on, doesn't the old look good sometimes? Be brave. Hang on. The new will settle down and eventually feel comfortable. Once the new has its place, nobody will long for the old.

The Jewish nation, once settled in the Promised Land, no longer yearned for the good old days of Egypt. Those days were gone forever. This transition for the Jewish people turned out to be a great blessing. What about the Egyptians? If you could have asked Egypt, they would have said that this transition was the greatest tribulation they had ever known. Remember while Egypt was troubled, the people of God were safe in Goshen. What was tribulation for one was a great blessing for the others. God was setting the stage for Israel to be released from bondage with the spoils of Egypt in their pockets.

From the fall of Adam until the deliverance of Israel from Egypt, the earth had never seen anything like this transition. God showed Himself as the defender of His people, and Israel flourished in God's glory.

Chapter XI

Transition #2

From the deliverance of Israel and the giving of the Law, the Jewish nation prospered for centuries. However, nothing as dramatic as that first time of deliverance ever occurred again in Israel's history.

Sadly, toward the end of the Calf (the Age of the Law), Israel once again found themselves in bondage. This time, however, they were not only in physical bondage to Rome, but also in spiritual bondage to their traditions. The glory of God that they once knew was covered up by their own traditions. Their longing for freedom and preeminence caused many nationalists to rise against the tyranny of Rome. Some even claimed to be the Messiah.

Remember that just prior to God's move, you can usually expect a reaction from darkness. This pre-transition move of darkness is an attempt to pull the energies of true worshippers away from God's plan and entice them in other directions. In the book of Acts, Gamaliel explained that the desire to be nationally comfortable again even caused Israel to miss their Messiah when He came. Their cries for deliverance were heard in heaven and answered, but in a way they hadn't dreamed.

This time instead of tapping a man on the shoulder and telling him what to do, God Himself entered the world bound in flesh and He set in motion the second of God's great transitions. As the fullness of time came, the increase of God's power was once again seen. God sent an agent of change to orchestrate the transition from the Law (Calf) to the Age of the Church (Son of man).

The ministry of Jesus was like no other before Him. Leaders marveled at His words and miraculous works. The divine crescendo peaked with Jesus' death, burial, resurrection, and the birthing of the Church with the fullness of the Holy Spirit. The heavenly glow of the glory of God stayed with the Church for some time after Pentecost. Favor to grow and mature was on the Church. Nothing could dampen the fire that the Holy Spirit lit. Everywhere Jesus was glorified and the Church grew.

Transition #2

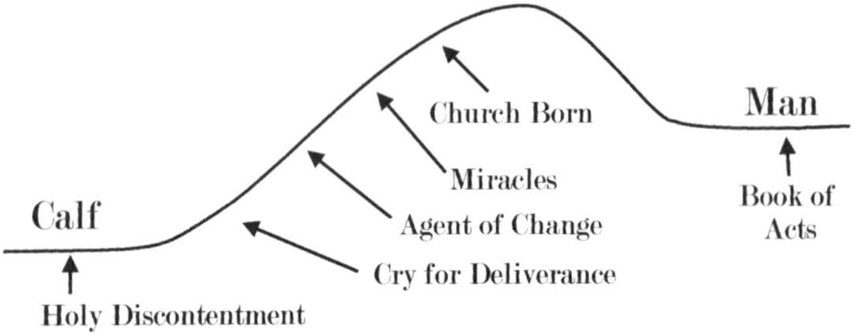

Again we see God holding man's hand through another change. When God moves mankind to another step in His progressive, redemptive plan, the power of God surges. Never before had this planet seen the wonderful works that confirmed Jesus' ministry. Not only were the dead raised, but He Himself came back from the grave and continued His ministry on earth until 10 days before the Holy Spirit came.

Was everybody glad to see Jesus? Did they welcome change with open arms? There were numerous attempts on His life before He actually laid it down at Calvary. Just as in Transition #1 when people in the wilderness were rebuked for their hardness of heart, Jesus accused modern Israel of the same sickness of heart. Did everyone make it through Transition #1? No, not many. Joshua and Caleb were the only two to make it all the way through. Did all the people make it through Transition #2? This time Acts tells us that thousands made this transition successfully.

Those who were previously servants of the Law were now servants of the Son of Man--Jesus. Ask any of those who made it through if they would now like to forsake grace and go back to the Law. Sadly, some did. Just as Israel in the wilderness longed for the leeks and onions of Egypt, a few Christians went back to the Law. However, the overwhelming majority found new freedom and once again experienced the glory of God in such a way that the Church exploded with growth and zeal.

Once the transition was complete and the Church was born and firmly planted, an old pattern began to emerge. Through the centuries, Christians began to get comfortable with the new. Once again we see traditions and familiarity draining the freshness of this new life. The glory and wondrous works that birthed the Church began fading. Just as Israel in Jesus' day spoke of the good old days of Moses and the Law, the Church of today talks about the good old days of Jesus' miracles and grace.

Just as Israel then was in bondage to the Law and needed deliverance into a better place, the Church of today is in bondage to the old and cries out for deliverance into a better place. This is not to say that there are not many churches, ministries, and individual believers who are hard at work helping the world find Christ. It is just that once again the time has come for change.

After all, if we will honestly evaluate the modern church, we must ask the question, "Is this all there is?." For many in the Church today it seems that there is no fresh revelation. In many churches nothing has changed in the last 10 to 20 years. Yet, the Holy Spirit's fragrance is still giving us encouragement that there is more that God has to reveal to the Church. When you begin to smell the new, it is difficult to be satisfied with the old.

As impossible as it may seem, after God's next step in His progressive plan of redemption, those of us who make it through Transition #3 (from the Man to the Eagle) will look back and say, "How did we ever survive under grace?".

Now don't throw rocks yet. Isn't that what the New Testament believers said when they looked back at the Law? Imagine 50 years before Christ someone standing in a synagogue and saying, "The day is coming when we will look back and say, 'How did we ever survive under the Law?'." God authorized the Law, yet it was incomplete in its ability to fully redeem man.

God authorized grace and the Age of the Son of Man, but there is a fourth beast that must be revealed to complete God's progressive plan of redemption. From this side, it may seem impossible. Remember how impossible the Promised Land must have seemed to those bound in Egypt. How impossible would the freedom and liberty the Church enjoys today have seemed to those bound by the Law? Just because some of the possibilities we will discuss may seem a little difficult for us to understand today, don't doubt God's ability to pull off some major changes in the next years ahead for the Church.

This brings us to the present in our journey. If my theory of the beasts in Revelation is accurate, we now find ourselves at the end of the Third Age and ready for a major transition into Age #4--the Eagle. Before we launch into our near future and eventual destiny, let's briefly review some vital points to build upon.

Chapter XII

What You Believe About Satan Is Important

Know your Enemy

The Christian today is challenged with a wide variety of opinions and information about Satan. Some teach that Satan is a defeated enemy that should simply be ignored, while others fear him to the point of being immobilized. Either extreme can leave a vulnerability in our planning for global conquest. In order to fight a good fight, there are some truths that we must never forget. The way we think determines how we act. If we believe that Calvary was the end of the story and Satan was totally and utterly defeated and no longer has any power, then we will live our life from that perspective. If Satan and all his plans and power were destroyed at Calvary, then somebody forgot to inform him. Our world today continues to decay socially. Sin, rebellion, and self are promoted as never before.

Others fear Satan to the point that they will never take a risk for righteousness. They don't want to confront darkness for fear that they will incur some demonic wrath. Their actions and beliefs send a message that darkness is stronger than light. Some believers fear a witch's curse more than they trust in a righteous man's prayer. Both are simply words backed by beliefs that are invested into a system of spiritual power. Your life and its decisions will be channeled into actions based on which system you believe is more powerful--darkness or light. You see, what you believe about Satan is important. The Scriptures call Satan the god of this world. He is the prince of the power of the air and rules from an invisible throne in heavenly places.

Is it reasonable to assume that God did not create seats of rulership over planet earth for Satan to sit on to rule mankind? Remember, Satan was supposed to be *Kabashed* by Adam. Satan rules today because he usurped (unrighteously tricked and took) from Adam the position of rulership which God created for man to rule. That means that before sin took Adam's place away, Adam was the god of this world. God's delegated authority placed Adam in the position of rulership and Satan stole it for himself.

How Does Satan Continue to Exist?

Is Satan self-sufficient? If he were an eternal creature who needed nothing to exist, he certainly would be as God. Satan, however, is a created being, and as such he needs something to feed on. Yes, even Satan must depend on something in God's creation from which he draws his very existence. Every created being requires something outside itself to be taken into itself in order to live. Bugs eat plants, birds eat bugs, cats eat birds, and so on. What does Satan eat? As a spiritual being, does he eat meat and potatoes? What is the secret ingredient that he takes into himself that keeps him alive?

The Scripture calls him a thief and a robber. Since sin has separated him from the source of life (a relationship with God), then he has only one way to draw what he needs from creation to exist. He must steal it. John 10:10 says that he is a thief, come but for to steal, to kill, and to destroy. Satan and his kingdom are on a feeding frenzy. He pulls the very life from mankind and consumes men's lives to exist.

All the good provision that God has intended for us is systematically siphoned off to keep darkness supplied. Darkness then uses against us what was intended for our good. As long as we are continually forced into a defensive posture, we are not nearly as effective. Satan's hit-and-run tactics are designed to keep us focused on mere survival and not on conquest.

As the Church awakens to their potential, imagine what will happen when we stand up and take back what, by Calvary, is ours. If you thought it was good being saved while Satan was stealing most of your heavenly provision, imagine what life will be like when you have at your disposal all heaven intends for you to have.

What Is Satan's Social Agenda?

Every earthly administration becomes known for its goals or programs that are implemented in order to move society along a certain path. The communists of history had stated goals to mold whole societies. In America, Democrats and Republicans are known by the social programs they are for or against. If Satan truly has taken control of the heavenly thrones and rules from them, then in time his social agenda will become evident as we observe its application. In other words, just what is he trying to accomplish and how effective is he at accomplishing his goals?

Remember, John 10:10 says that he is a thief come but for to steal, to kill, and to destroy. He is as a roaring lion seeking whom he may devour. When we look at the last 6,000 years of human history, I think it is clear that the agenda of the thief, murderer, and destroyer is right on schedule. You see, when God rules, everything lives and thrives with purpose and meaning. When Satan rules, everything dies in despair.

As soon as Satan took over, the planet with all of its ecosystems and social order began to die. Man's life span shortened drastically. Disease not only attacked mankind, but it attacked the plant world as well. Insects destroyed crops. Hatred divided mankind with suspicions. Today pollution and environmental mismanagement paints a gloomy future if you don't know the marvelous, redemptive plan God has for this old world.

God's plan to set things right again began when Adam sinned. Under Satan's rule, society is slowly drained of hope for a brighter future. All of creation now fights against man's success. Man now contends with the thorns, briers, thistles, and the sweat of the brow. Before, when Adam ruled, all of creation cooperated with man's success. Not anymore. However, when Jesus died sinless and passed through the heavens renewing our access to heaven, the plan was set into motion to recapture the thrones of rulership over planet earth.

Chapter XIII

The Progressive "Anointing" of the Agents of Change

Jewish history honors Moses (agent of change in Transition #1) for the role he played in that first great transition. Without his faithfulness to intercede for Israel, who knows how much longer and more difficult the deliverance of Israel might have been. From the burning bush to the rod becoming a serpent, Moses struggled with his own humanity. The thought of standing before Pharaoh was not something he looked forward to. He reasoned with God that he may not be the best choice. Moses had to deal with his own fear of going back to Egypt and confronting the power that was enslaving Israel. However, in the end, Moses drew deeply from the strength of God and found his place in God's plan. Israel came out of Egypt a victorious, blessed, prospered people. The plagues that God brought on Egypt not only weakened Egypt's hold, but they also strengthened Moses' leadership over Israel.

All of us want to be used of God until He tells us what it is He wants us to do. Many times the revelation of God's will staggers us. Even if we don't stagger from unbelief, we may find ourselves staggering from the sheer size of the plan. God thinks big. Whatever it is God involves you in, it will definitely expand you.

Moses found himself in a career change at age 80. He no longer tended sheep on the backside of the desert; he was now leading Israel from Egypt to the Promised Land.

Talk about confidence-building experiences. When you stand as God's representative and God backs you up with His ability, your confidence surges. Moses, over and over again, experienced God backing him with signs, wonders, and miracles. The world had never seen anything like it.

Why was this power display so important? If the nation of Israel hadn't seen the power of God, they may not have had the confidence necessary to begin their journey. If Egypt had not seen the power of God, they may not have let Israel go. This display of power moved a nation, and in the process, secured Moses' place as the deliverer for whom Israel cried out.

Once established in the Law and the Promised Land, Israel flourished. Moses was honored in the culture, in history, and in the hearts of the people. As wonderful as Moses' life was, however, it pales in comparison to the life and ministry of Jesus. I think it goes without saying that the impact of Jesus' life, ministry, and miracles on the Jewish nation and the rest of the world was certainly greater than that of Moses'. Have you wondered why it was important that Jesus' life and ministry overshadowed that of Moses'?

What if we in today's Church looked back at those two lives and decided that Moses really did more than Jesus? If we viewed the teachings of Moses more relevant and his miracles more powerful, then today we would be followers of Moses and Jesus' role in spiritual history would be diminished.

Jesus came to move us from the Law to Grace. If His life had not outshined Moses' life, we might still be followers of the Law today. We might be singing, "To be like Moses, to be like Moses, all I ask is to be like him." Thank God that Jesus' life and teachings have captivated true worshippers in a way that has pulled them past

Moses' teachings and to a higher level of relationship with God.

We don't dislike or mistrust Moses, we simply see clearly, by the greater anointing on Jesus' life, that God was moving His followers forward in His redemptive plan. The law in our hearts is better than commandments on stone. Forgiveness and cleansing from sin is better than simply covering our sins.

But now we find ourselves moving toward the end of the Church Age and the words of Jesus ring out,

> **Verily, verily, I say unto you, "He who believes on Me, the works that I do shall he do also; and greater works than these shall he do; because I go unto My Father."**
>
> **John 14:12**

Answer this question honestly: Have you seen greater works than Jesus did? Oh, I know that some teach that the quantity of works that the Church has done in the last 2,000 years is greater than Jesus did in His lifetime. However, I don't think that is an appropriate answer.

When you hold Moses' ministry up to Jesus' in comparison, there certainly is no argument that Jesus had the greater works. The question remains: Where can we find a ministry that, when compared to that of Jesus', we could classify it as being greater? Remember those were Jesus' own words, not mine. How can it be?

> **Verily, verily, I say unto you, He that believes on Me, the works that I do shall he do also; and greater works than these shall he do; because I go unto my Father.**
>
> **John 14:12**

I believe that the transition the Church is about to go through, from the Age of the Church (Son of Man) to the Millennium (the Eagle), will call for an unprecedented outpouring of the miraculous power of God. The agent of change in Transition #3 will experience something never before seen by this world. Something is coming so powerful that the saints will be delivered from their fear of change. This deliverance will allow them to embrace the challenge. When the agent of change stands in that day under that anointing, the words of Jesus will finally be fulfilled.

Chapter XIV

Transition #3--Tribulation or Opportunity

When the time has come for some things, the markers seem to be evident everywhere. The automobile was developed in America and in Europe almost simultaneously without either knowing the other was working on the project. Three different groups worked at the same time to develop the airplane. When something's time has come, it seems nothing can stop it.

When it was time for Israel to be delivered from Egypt, God's people were in bondage making bricks without straw. Their situation of need caused them to call out to God for deliverance. Egypt was so bad, almost anything else looked good. Israel was ready for a change. They cried out for change. God sent an agent of change (Moses). God, with miracles, confirmed He was behind the change, and Israel moved to the Promised Land.

Toward the end of the Age of the Law, God's people once again found themselves in bondage. This time they were in bondage to the same Law that had started out to be such a blessing. Two thousand years of interpretation and reinterpretation had expanded the application of the Law to the point that it was choking the spiritual life out of the nation with so many *do's* and *don'ts*. Israel was no longer liberated by the Law, but rather was now in crushing servitude to a code that was incapable of giving life. They were now making spiritual bricks without straw as well. On top of this, Rome had conquered Israel and further reinforced their need for a change. Once again, Israel was ready for a change. They cried out for change. The prophets predicted a Messiah and in their worship Israel cried to God for a deliverer. God responded by sending an agent of change (Jesus). God once again confirmed by undeniable miracles that He was behind the change. The result was that those who believed moved into a totally new dimension of living. The Age of the Church was born.

Basically, for the last 2,000 years, not much has changed. Very little progress or improvement has been made since the completion of the book of Acts. Today, if someone is saved, speaks in other tongues, prophesies, casts out devils, raises the dead, has visions from heaven, delivers the word to kings, and gets into trouble with the authorities for his faith, we might describe such a one as a mature, sold-out Christian.

If all of that were true, all that we have seen is a duplication of the book of Acts. And if that was all there was to Christianity, we would not see the turnover we do in churches. People have been exposed to Acts' Christianity for centuries. I propose to you that, as we near the end of this age, a holy discontentment is rising among the people of God.

The part of the Church that I hear from is beginning to voice a deep hunger for the next event on God's calendar. Many have grown weary of the same predictable worship from week to week. I hear them saying, "When will things change? When do we get to win? What's next?" To hear some ministers tell it, there is nothing left to be fulfilled or work to be done before Jesus returns. If everything is finished, then what is holding up the plan? Let's take an objective look at some possibilities.

Who Will Start the Tribulation (Transition #3)?

The traditional answer to this question is that at some point in the future, when the Church is raptured out of the earth, the devil will descend on planet earth with a vengeance and tear this place apart. This feeling that the devil can't wait to get his hands on new believers and cut off their heads may be a little misplaced. Tell me, if you were the devil, would you want to start the tribulation? Surely, the devil can read. Revelation clearly spells out the fact that the tribulation is the beginning of the end of Satan's rebellious rulership. The book of Revelation, however you interpret it, tells us that Satan is bound for 1,000 years and after that is loosed for a little season, then cast into the Lake of Fire. If I were the devil, I certainly wouldn't want that sequence of events to begin. In fact, if I were the devil, I would use every tool at my disposal to delay the beginning of those events as long as I could.

Certainly, everything is in God's capable hands. The times and seasons of all things are His to manage. But could it be that God Himself is looking for a signal in human history? Is there some point of growth or understanding that man must attain before God moves? After all, remember, if God moves before we are ready by faith to embrace what He is up to, we may well misinterpret God's plan and miss His intended provision. Isn't the millennium going to be a better place for the saints? Doesn't God want the best for His people? If all of that is true, and it is, then what is God waiting for? Maybe He is waiting for us.

Who Started the Tribulation (Transition #1)?

The Scriptures clearly state in Exodus 3:7 that God saw Israel's affliction and **heard their cry**. In verse 8, He states that for this reason, "I have come down to deliver them." God was moved by the cries of His people. Over and over, throughout biblical history, we find that God moved in response to the cries of people. More often than not, this was the case.

Remember that while real tribulation embraced Egypt, the people of God were blessed and released to their destiny, the Promised Land (Ex.12:35-36 tells how Israel spoiled Egypt).

What About Tribulation (Transition #2)?

Certainly, Israel was in a difficult place. Bound physically by Rome and spiritually by their own traditions, their discontentment begged for change. While the Scriptures do state that God sent His Son in the fullness of time, we ask ourselves, "How did time get full?."

I strongly believe that a holy discontentment precedes God's move. Without that hunger to know God in a fresh way many would miss the benefits Heaven had planned. Hunger sets the table for the meal God has prepared. While many of the Saducees, Pharisees, and others in places of authority rejected Christ's ministry, the multitudes flocked to His healing words and hands. At the grassroots level the holy discontentment was clearly present. God, seeing the time was ripe to inject the message of the Kingdom into fertile hearts, sent Jesus in the fullness of time.

Tribulation the Great (Transition #3)

To move from the Age of the Church to the Millennium (the Eagle), God needs certain criteria to be present. First, a holy discontentment with the spiritual status quo must rise. The Church, or at least a segment of the Church, must understand that there is more needed from heaven to see the kingdom come here as it is in heaven. When hungry hearts cry out and say, "Surely this isn't all that God has for His people," then the time is near.

> **Blessed are they who do hunger and thirst after righteousness; for they shall be filled.**
>
> **Matthew 5:6**

This holy discontentment means the hungry are ready to accept change. They long for more of God in their hearts and in their world. I believe that in response to these hungry hearts, God will send an agent of change that will be the catalyst to move the Church to the true "New Age"--the Millennium. Is it any wonder that the very term "new age" has been stolen by the "spiritual" fringe and they have played with every wacky idea imaginable? Remember, Satan is a liar and will attempt to discredit every genuine move of God before it begins. The real is always preceded by the false.

If it is our hunger that will eventually set things in motion, then if you were Satan and knew that this would be the beginning of your end, how would you stop or delay the inevitable? The truth is that when believers see clearly the glory of the Millennium, they will hunger and thirst for the new to the point that nothing will stop them from moving toward their promised land. The devil has lied to the Church for years about the tribulation. If he can keep the Church comfortable enough, then the hunger for change will never come. If he can keep the Church fearful enough, it will lose heart and give up before the battle ever begins. The motivation to survive keeps Satan scrambling. Never forget that when tribulation finally does come, Satan has the most to lose and we have the most to gain.

Remember, what was tribulation for Egypt was blessing to Israel. The time of transition just ahead of us is the greatest opportunity the people of God have ever known. While the harvest of souls is occurring, heaven is also judging the wicked and hard hearted.

Are there hard times ahead? Obviously there are. Shall we fear what's ahead? Perfect love for the souls of men and the plan of God will cast out all fear of what the devil can do. When we value what God has planned more than we fear what Satan can do, fear loses its ability to control us.

Just because the devil has puffed himself up to appear invincible, don't let that appearance fool you. Somewhere the insignificant-appearing Davids of the

Kingdom must take on the arrogant Goliaths of darkness. David stood up to the giant and said, *...for who is this uncircumcised Philistine, that he should defy the armies of the living God* (1 Samuel 17:26)? Paraphrased he declared, "You can't talk about the God of Israel like that. I refuse to let you." David lost his fear of the enemy and took off Goliath's head. In the same way, the Sons of God (the manchild of Rev. 12 and the agent of change in Transition #3) will stand against Satan and say, "Not anymore you don't. Who do you think you are anyway? You can no longer rule by intimidation. We overcome you by the blood of the Lamb and the word of our testimony."

Now what can our enemy threaten us with? Nothing. When we realize that Christ gave us the victory over Satan at Calvary and that the Lord of the battle Himself fights with us, there is no enemy that can stand before us.

> **...and they loved not their lives unto the death.**
>
> **Revelation 12:11**

When God's people have hungry hearts, clear vision of the future, see the opportunity rather than the problem, and lose their fear of the devil, they will engage the enemy as never before. You see for the past 6,000 years, mankind has served under the cruel rulership of a thief who has stolen the provisions of God and consumed them in his own lust. When the Church clearly sees the genuine opportunity to end Satan's reign as the god of this world, you tell me how he will be able to hold them back any longer. The great lie is about to be unmasked and the Church is about to understand that we have been given true power over all the works of the devil. That includes his power as prince of the power of the air.

Romans 8 speaks of all of nature groaning and travailing, waiting for the manifestation of the sons of God (the agent of change of Transition #3). It's no wonder that the devil is seeking whom he may devour. He wants to destroy us before we awaken to our destiny. Jesus died to restore to us Adam's authority. He paid with His life to give us back what we lost. Now it is time for us to reclaim that which has already been paid for. Satan rules today only by deception. He sits on invisible thrones usurped from Adam that are our birthright. Once the truth of these words find a home deep inside your belief system, you will cry out with the others who understand.

"Move over Satan; you're in my seat!"

The seat of rulership over planet earth belongs to Adam's seed, not to darkness. What is the Millennium anyway? It is a time during which Satan is locked up and we ***Rule and Reign*** with Christ for 1,000 years. We truly are destined for the throne. Ephesians 2:6 says that we are seated together in heavenly places in Christ Jesus. When you lose your fear of the bully, you will take back your destiny and you, along with all of nature, will be blessed. The death rulership of Satan will be broken off planet earth and the life rulership of heaven will once again cause this place to thrive as the garden of God.

Chapter XV

The Hinderer Versus Agent of Change #3

> **And now you know what withholds that he might be revealed in his time. For the mystery of iniquity does already work: only he who now lets (or *hinders*) will let (or *hinder*), until he be taken out of the way.**
>
> **II Thessalonians 2:6-7**
>
> (Parentheses added for explanation)

For years many have taught that the hinderer is the Holy Spirit. They say that the Holy Spirit's job is to hold back evil through the Church in the world and that when the Church is raptured out, the devil has the earth to do with as he wants. Oh, it will be awful and you certainly wouldn't want to be around when it really gets bad. I can see why the rapture would be a teaching of great comfort to people who believe this way.

If the Holy Spirit's job is to hold the devil back, then you look at our world's condition and tell me what kind of job He is doing. The world is getting worse by the day. I assure the Holy Spirit is not a failure. I don't believe the Church is a failure either. Rather, I think this whole passage of Scripture has been misunderstood.

In the discussions of the previous chapter, you tell me who has the most to gain from hindering (vs. 8). Who doesn't want the wicked one to be revealed? The wicked one. You see it is Satan and his lies who are hindering the things of God only because he is still the prince of the power of the air. He is using every trick to prolong his rule. Rev. 12 is the story of II Thes 2:7--when he is taken out of the way. He sits as the toll keeper of the heavens, hindering spiritual rulership of Adam's seed. The thief continues to steal our stuff and to lie to us about what is coming. Somebody must "take him out" of the way. It is only after Revelation 12 that there is an antichrist on planet earth: *and then shall that wicked {one} be revealed* (2 Thes 2:8).

Take hold of this: When Adam sinned, Satan was released into the heavens and man became Satan's prisoner, locked in the physical on planet earth. When redeemed man (the sons of God) takes him out of the way, we then are released to our destiny and he is once again confined to the physical.

How do we know that the redeemed are part of the heavenly army of Revelation 12? It says they overcame him (Satan) by the blood of the Lamb and the word of their testimony. Angels don't qualify for this description. Only redeemed men and women can overcome him by the blood of the Lamb and the word of their testimony.

A segment (the manchild) of the Church (the sun clothed woman) will awaken to their Adamic potential which includes freedom from the physical world. The Scriptures have many examples of mankind temporarily stepping out of the physical world. Perhaps the clearest statement was made by Paul in 2 Cor 12:3 when he said, *I knew such a man, (whether in the body, or out of the body, I cannot tell: God knows).* Paul and many others before and after him have been privileged to venture outside the confines of the flesh. It seems obvious that if man lost dominion, it will be redeemed man, empowered by Calvary's provision, who will confront Satan with the armies of heaven and regain what Adam lost. It says he is cast down to earth by this army and is upset because he knows he has but a little season. It is only after the events of Revelation 12 that we have an antichrist. Tell me, if a segment of the Church participates in the dethroning of Satan in the heavenlies, and see him cast down to earth, do you think that group would fear Satan any longer? That is why he gets so angry because he is once again limited to the physical world. He now knows he has a short time left until he is finished. The lie that he is someone to be feared is unmasked and his fate is sealed. Only after he is imprisoned in physical form will he be destroyed.

If the Church fully understood this glorious season, there would be all night prayer meetings calling for the tribulation. Redeemed Adams would war in the heavenlies to regain their rightful place of rulership. When antichrist is revealed, a victory shout should rise from the Church because we also know he has but a little season. We should see the glory of the Millennium on the horizon and be energized to fight the good fight and keep the faith delivered to the saints.

Chapter XVI

So...What About the Rapture?

I hope by now you are beginning to lose your fear of what is coming and see the glorious opportunity to set in motion events that will truly bless all of mankind. Once the fear of the devil is gone, the security blanket of a pre-tribulation rapture is no longer quite as attractive. If what I have presented makes sense to you, why would we want to run from the very destiny Christ died to purchase for us?

So is there a rapture? Of course there is. As I Thes 4:16-18 clearly states, we will be caught up to meet the Lord in the air:

> **For the Lord Himself shall descend from heaven with a shout, with the voice of the archangel, and with the trump of God: and the dead in Christ shall rise first:**
>
> **Then we which are alive and remain shall be caught up together with them in the clouds, to meet the Lord in the air: and so shall we ever be with the Lord.**
>
> **1 Thessalonians 4:16-17**

There are three questions that remain. First when will this event occur? We find the answer to the first question in Matthew.

> **Immediately after the tribulation of those days shall the sun be darkened, and the moon shall not give her light, and the stars shall fall from heaven, and the powers of the heavens shall be shaken:**
>
> **And then shall appear the sign of the Son of man in heaven: and then shall all the tribes of the earth mourn, and they shall see the Son of man coming in the clouds of heaven with power and great glory.**
>
> **And He shall send His angels with a great sound of a trumpet, and they shall gather together His elect from the four winds, from one end of heaven to the other.**
>
> **Matthew 24:29-31**

Second, since we are now with Him, where is He going? Zech 14 and Revelation 19 are parallel passages describing the same sequence of events. Zech says:

> **And His feet shall stand in that day upon the mount of Olives, which is before Jerusalem on the east...**
>
> **Zechariah 14:4**

If you read the context of Zech Chapters 12-14, there is no doubt this is referring to Jesus' second coming to Jerusalem, just as the angels told the disciples He would.

Third, what is He going to do?

And I saw heaven opened, and behold a white horse; and He that sat upon him was called Faithful and True, and in righteousness He does judge and make war.

His eyes were as a flame of fire, and on His head were many crowns; and He had a name written, that no man knew, but He Himself.

And He was clothed with a vesture dipped in blood: and His name is called The Word of God

And the armies which were in heaven followed Him upon white horses, clothed in fine linen, white and clean.

And out of His mouth goes a sharp sword, that with it He should smite the nations: and He shall rule them with a rod of iron: and He treads the winepress of the fierceness and wrath of Almighty God.

Revelation 19:11-15

For the final battle of the tribulation, Jesus comes with the armies of heaven (the saints who have died and gone before us) and joins the Church on earth (those of us standing against Satan here) to destroy those who have gathered against Jerusalem. This is the Battle of Armageddon. A 200,000,000 soldier army is destroyed by the word coming from Jesus' mouth.

From the above verses we understand that Jesus isn't coming in the clouds to meet the elect until the end of the tribulation and that when He does come, He's coming to

Jerusalem. Jesus isn't coming again and again. He is coming again (once). When He returns to earth, it is to rule and reign 1,000 years in Jerusalem.

You tell me. When the Church presses the battle to the end and invites Jesus back to earth, the Scriptures say He comes in the clouds. As Jesus takes a lap around the planet on His way to Jerusalem and Armageddon and we see Him, the Scriptures tell us that when we see Him, we will be like Him. Finally, we too will be delivered from the limitations of a physical existence. If you have fought the good fight and your King returns to bring the final victory and you are no longer limited to the physical, wouldn't you rush forward to meet Him in the air? In that moment, in the twinkling of an eye, we will be changed and freed from the physical. Yes, I believe there is a rapture. Not a rapture to rescue the Church from a crushing wave of wickedness, but a rapturous moment of rejoicing and ecstasy to welcome earth's returning King.

> **...The kingdoms of this world they have become the kingdoms of our Lord, and of His Christ, and He shall reign for ever and ever.**
>
> **Revelation 11:15**

And I heard as it were the voice of a great multitude, and as the voice of many waters, and as the voice of mighty thunderings, saying, Alleluia: for the Lord God omnipotent reigns.

Revelation 19:6

Once this third transition is complete, mankind along with all of creation, will be delivered into the glorious liberty of the sons of God. The pain and inconvenience of this climactic change will be swallowed up in the joy of Jesus' rulership. Bring on the Eagle!

Chapter XVII

Beast #4--The Eagle

Jesus' first miracle was turning water into wine. When the wine was delivered to the governor of the wedding, he told the bridegroom that he had saved the best wine for last. In the same way, God has saved the best of His redemptive plan for last. Looking back at the Ages of the Lion, the Calf, and the Man-Beast is fairly easy. All we have to do is observe what happened and was reported. Looking forward to the Age of the Eagle is more difficult because it is not all spelled out for us in black and white. However, the Scriptures do provide some glimpse of what is ahead. In the same way that Isaiah told us about Jesus' life and ministry, the prophets also let us peek into the future once again.

Let me try to put the bait on the hook. If you can see the reward clearly enough, then whatever price is asked will not be too great. Do you remember where we began this journey? I was wondering what it would be like to live in a perfect world. Adam was given that perfect place, but it didn't even pass on to the next generation.

How I have longed for that place to come back again. The Millennium is as close as we can get for at least 1,000 years.

Imagine a world where all our leaders are in covenant with the righteous government of Jerusalem. The Scriptures tell us that Jesus will return and rule the nations with a rod of iron. If the rulers of nations are not doing what is right, they will answer to the throne in Jerusalem, not NATO or the United Nations. National injustice will be subjugated to heavenly authority. There will be no room for any more Hitlers. Leaders will serve to the good of their people. When the righteous rule the nation is blessed. Today the deep distrust of leadership is a cancer eating away the partnership between people and their government. When that division grows, societies deteriorate and every evil work abounds. Wouldn't it be wonderful if the respect and honor leaders once earned could return? Soon it will.

Imagine a world void of prejudice. It is so unjust for people's potential to be limited by something they cannot control. Often before someone is given a chance, the decision is already made as to how far they can go. When the Kingdom comes to earth, then there will be neither male nor female, bond nor free, Jew nor Greek, black nor white, First World nor Third World. In that day, honor and opportunity will be given based on commitment to the Kingdom. Having friends in the right places won't buy privileges in that world. That may not be the case today. Soon it will be.

Imagine the world with nature healed. This may be one of the most dramatic changes of all. Romans 8 says that all of nature groans and travails waiting for the sons of God to take the place back. While many look into the future with gloom and doom, it has been my privilege to peek through the veil. I am personally aware of technologies that are about to radically change our whole way of living. These "Millennial Technologies" address many of our most glaring environmental challenges. In that world food will be abundant, energy will be free, transportation to any place on earth will take less than one hour, communication will be available to everyone, and sickness will all but disappear as the earth heals. Pollution will disappear and water will be abundant and clean. The animal world will sign a peace treaty with man. Housing will be available to all. Imagine the most beautiful garden or golf course or landscape you have ever seen and then paint the whole world with it. Soon it will be.

Imagine a world where you are free to create. Perhaps the biggest curse to be removed is to live by the sweat of your brow. Not that I am against work. I am not. Work is perhaps one of the greatest gifts God has ever given us. What is not wonderful, however, is to be forced to toil day after day, not doing what you were created to do or what brings you real joy, but rather, what you have to do to get by. If Satan keeps us in a survival mentality, we can never be creative enough to threaten him. In the world to come, work will be a joy because with our basic needs met, we will work with God as partners in His creation. Work will be challenging, rewarding, exciting. If it isn't that way for you yet, soon it will be.

Imagine a world where you feel safe and secure. People often ask me if I am afraid of traveling so often to Africa. Most of this book has been written in Sierre Leone and Ghana. I have to honestly say I feel safer in Africa than I do in many places in the US and Europe. It is awful to live with locks on your doors and to be suspicious of your neighbors. In New York City, in a recent strike of sanitation workers, people didn't know what to do with their trash that was piling up. Several creative folks gift wrapped their trash and left it on the front seat of their unlocked cars. They were so confident in the depravity of man, and for good reason; their trash was faithfully stolen from their car within minutes after it was parked.

The sense of family and partnership is sorely missed in our world today. With the return of community values and service to others, our houses won't need four locks on the doors, security alarms, and a guard dog. Regaining trust in our fellow man may seem far off if you look at the present. The world to come will certainly be a different place. Soon it will be.

Imagine a world where you could ask Jesus questions face to face. To have Jesus here will make all of the above possible. All the questions, inequities, imbalances, and disorders of our present society will be submitted to His loving fairness and rulership. This one possibility alone should cause us to rise to the occasion of this hour. "Even so come quickly, Lord Jesus!"

You see, as much as Jesus wants to return, He cannot until the next fullness of time. We must first have a transition because Jesus' rule in Jerusalem only begins after the tribulation. If it is truly in our hand to start things in motion by our hunger for the world to be set right, then you may come to the same conclusion as many others. **"Satan, move over."** It is time for Adam's seed to be restored. If there is a price for the Millennium and that price is the tribulation, then let us pay the price.

In the same way that Jesus looked past the cross despising the shame and for the joy that was set before Him said, "Let Me pay the price," can we do any less? I pray you can begin now to see through the dark glass of Transition #3 to the glorious peace of the Eagle.

> **But they that wait upon the Lord shall renew their strength; they shall mount up with wings as eagles; They shall run, and not be weary; they shall walk, and not faint.**
>
> **Isaiah 40:31**

Summary--Age of the Eagle

The Millennium is a season of healing for the earth and all who live in it. As we approach the end of this season, we are ever closer to the full restoration of all things.

In the ages to come, the curse is finally lifted. Only when Adam's loss is fully restored can we see man's full potential realized. We then will once again enter into God's timeless dimension of eternal life.

Key Elements of the Age of the Eagle

1. Length of the Age - 1,000 years from Jesus' return to the earth to the coming of the New Jerusalem
2. Rule of the Age - Jesus' rule from Jerusalem through His delegated authority in the saints
3. Motivation for Transition - Destruction, clearing the way for the New Jerusalem to come to earth
4. Agent of Change - The Sons of God
5. Length of Transition - Unknown

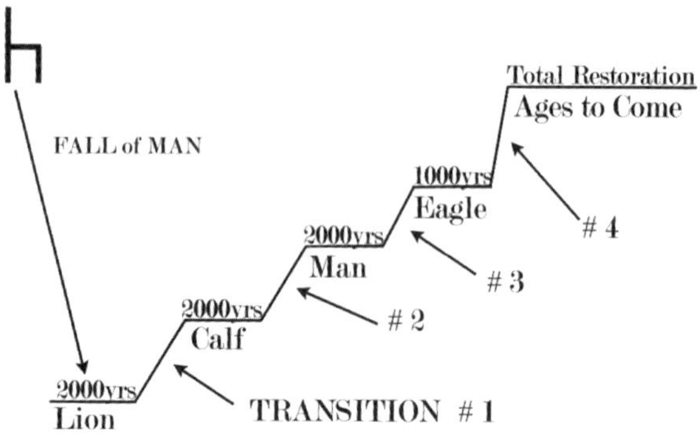

Chapter XVIII

Ages to Come--Full Restoration

After the Eagle--Then What?

Once the saints complete the Millennium and the world goes through the judgment, the most wondrous event of all occurs. The full redemptive mantle of Adam's authority is restored to mankind and the recreated earth receives the New Jerusalem where God and the Lamb will live forever. Now we are finally back where Adam started.

God and man are again in full fellowship and can walk again together in the cool of the evening. The physical and spiritual worlds are once again united. So now back to one of our first questions. Now that we are fully redeemed and no longer limited to the physical, what are we to do? In other words, what is it that Adam was to do that remains undone?

If Adam had never sinned and none of his offspring had ever sinned, how many people would be alive on earth today? Remember, no children would have died young. No wombs would have been barren. No flood or war or plague would have destroyed entire generations. And for all we know, Adam and Eve would still be having children. The answer is easily in the hundreds of billions or trillions. Do you think God needs all these workers to tend His garden? That would be one big garden. I am certain that God was only able to give Adam the beginning instructions of their relationship before sin created the great divide.

Remember, Adam had access to the spiritual world and so will his seed. Whatever God has in mind, be certain of this, our destiny is beyond anything we could ask or think. Earth in the future ages will be home base for activities assigned to us as God's ambassadors throughout the universe. At a later date and the Lord willing, these possibilities will be further explored in another book, The New Jerusalem.

> **And has raised us up together, and made us sit together in heavenly places in Christ Jesus; That in the ages to come He might show the exceeding riches of His grace in His kindness toward us through Christ Jesus.**
>
> **Ephesians 2:6-7**

In conclusion, let me remind you of my prayer in the introduction. I write this with the prayer that these discoveries will leave you forever changed and challenged to invest the rest of your life in this glorious quest. May God add His divine wisdom to this feeble attempt to unfold His mysteries. God bless you all.

So, which door do you choose:
Abraham's Blessings or Adam's Authority?